A
Fraction
of
Darkness

by Linda Pastan

A
Fraction
of
Darkness

Poems
by
Linda
Pastan

W · W · NORTON & COMPANY · *New York · London*

Acknowledgments
The Agni Review; Antaeus; The Atlantic Monthly; The Brockport Forum; Crosscurrents; Devil's Millhopper, Fiddlehead, The Georgia Review; Midstream; The Missouri Review; MSS; New England Review/Bread Loaf Quarterly; The New Republic; Pennsylvania Review; Ploughshares; Poetry; Poetry Miscellany; Poetry Now; Science '84; Tendril; Tri Quarterly; The Virginia Quarterly Review; The Washingtonian; Woman Poet: The South.

Published simultaneously in Canada by Penguin Books Canada Ltd, 2801 John Street, Markham, Ontario L3R 1B4
Printed in the United States of America.
The text of this book is composed in Optima. Composition and manufacturing by The Maple-Vail Book Manufacturing Group.

First Edition

Library of Congress Cataloging in Publication Data
Pastan, Linda, 1932–
    A fraction of darkness.

    I. Title.
PS3566.A775F7   1985   811'.54   85–4879

ISBN 0-393-02212-9

ISBN 0-393-30251-2 pbk

W. W. Norton & Company, Inc., 500 Fifth Avenue, New York, N.Y. 10110
W. W. Norton & Company Ltd., 37 Great Russell Street, London WC1B 3NU

1 2 3 4 5 6 7 8 9 0

For Ira

Contents

Our share of night to bear,
Our share of morning. . . .

Emily Dickinson

She . . . thought about the beautiful sentence
she had read in a translation of Dante's
account of their fatal kiss: "that day they read
no more." . . . Reading interrupted by kissing
and followed by death seemed to her an
entirely natural progression.

Anita Brookner, Providence

1. In the Kingdom of Midas

Overture

This is the way
it begins: the small
sure voice of the woodwind
leads us down a path brocaded
with colored leaves,
deep into a forest
we almost remember.
And though the percussions
have no exact equivalent,
soon we will find ourselves
thinking of weather—
a cold front rumbling in—
or of applause,
not for the self
but for someone we watch
bowing at the edge
of a pond whose waters,
like the cello's
darkest waters, part
letting the melody
slip through. This theme
presents itself so shyly
that when it returns full grown,
though it plucks
the live nerve of recollection
we will hear it
as if for the first time.
Make no mistake, this is only
music, shading with evening
into a minor key.
Whole flocks of birds rush up
spreading their night wings
as the harpist, that angel
who guarded the gates
in strict black, sweeps
her arm from E to G to high C,
and the bowing stranger
lifts his wand, letting
the curtains part.

In the Kingdom of Midas

If you follow the sun
from room to room,
wading in the pools
of light spilled
by that tawny,
molten river,

if you move all day
from east
to west, from kitchen
to study to bed,
by afternoon you'll see
the bedposts touched

and changed to sheaves of wheat,
and the children born
and nourished there will be
golden tongued
and golden headed.

For you the moon
has always been
the pale,
homely sister.
You tell your rosary
in saffron beads of light,

and though one day
you'll drown
in shade, the sun
will leave its heavy coins
on your closed lids
forever.

Suffocation: for RJP

In Chekhov's *Three Sisters,* everyone
is infected with terminal boredom.
When Irena says her soul is like a locked
piano without a key, I want
to tell her that playing the piano too
the fingers can wander up and down
the scales, going nowhere.
And when the talk leads always back
to Moscow, where she longs to be,
I wish I could remind Olga
of the cold, unyielding streets
where even the ice hardens to the color
of stone. Sitting here, watching
someone I love slowly die,
I see how anguish and boredom
can be married for years,
an ill-assorted couple, suffocating
in each other's arms.
I watched Masha at the curtain call, the tears
still streaming down her face
as she moved from one self
to the other through the wall
of applause, a kind of backwards birth.
And I wondered where all that feeling
came from if not some deep pool
where one can be dragged and dragged
beneath the surface but never quite drown.
Russia . . . I thought, Russia . . . a country
my grandfather thought he had escaped from
but which he wore always
like the heavy overcoat in the story
by Gogol, or the overcoat he wrapped me in
one night when the grown-ups kept on talking,
and I shivered and yawned in an ecstasy
of boredom that made my childhood
seem a vast continent I could only escape from
hidden in a coat, in steerage, and at great risk.

Japanese Lantern

After dreaming for years
over the black and white pages
of Katsura Palace,
we ordered a stone lantern
from Japan
and placed it in the garden
among American hollies
and an Austrian pine.
Next spring we'll prune the pine
the Japanese way, snipping
the clusters of new growth
that are like the short, stiff brooms
that Japanese women use
to clear Katsura's paths.
Tonight outlined in snow
our path is Japanese.
An animal has wandered by
leaving its tracks like ideographs
we cannot read,
although they lead somewhere
deep and familiar
in our woods.
Even these trees are textured
like the tree trunks
in the woodblock print
we hung over the bed. The eye is led
down needled paths
to a lantern almost like ours
with two lit windows.
At one a woman loosens her kimono.
At the other a man bends
over a book—Katsura perhaps,
where from the moon-viewing platform
something the size
of an almond can be seen
aslant in the sky.
When the lantern goes out
that moon will be broken
into a thousand fragments
and translated here
as snow.

At the Still Point

In April,
sitting on the deck
of this house
as on the deck of a great ship,
my fingers caught
between the pages of a book,
I watch the horizon
turn slowly
green, smell
the bent cherry unloading
its spiced cargo
at my feet.
The trees stretch
in the soft wind
as if they had been
merely asleep,
as if they had never known
any other leaves
but these.
What was lost in winter
remains lost. But
once again the wind flips
the pages of the book
like surf, delicately
backwards, and we start again
at the first chapter,
where just at the edge of sight
an ambiguous bee hangs
on the blossoms,
its ancient sting
almost forgotten.

Realms of Gold

1. Recess

I used to think
the cover of a book
was a door I could pull shut
after me,
that I was as safe
between pages
as between the clean sheets
of my bed at home.
The children in those books
were not like me.
They had the shine
of bravery or luck,
and their stories had endings.
But when Miss Colton called
"Yoo Hoo, Third Grade,"
and I had to come running,
the book suddenly
slippery under my arm, sometimes
those children ran with me.

2. The Quarrel

What are you doing?
he asks, and I turn a page,
then another.
Are you still reading?
And I pile page
after page, like sandbags,
between us.
I'm going to tear
that book out of your hands,
he says, but I don't hear him,
the sound of pages turning
is like a far train approaching,
and Anna has just
entered the station.

3. Final Instructions

When the time comes,
make my grave
with clean sheets
and a comforter of flowers.
If you come to call, rest
against the stone
which will lean like a bookend
over my head. Make yourself
at home there.
Read to me!

Donatello's Magdalene
wood sculpture, 15th Century

Old woman,
enrobed in nothing
but faith
and strands of chiseled hair,
the living tree once hid
those gnarled limbs, that face
worn to its perfect bones
which has seen everything.

Hag of articulate wood,
before Donatello found you
how many leaves did you watch
detach themselves
from your twigged fingers,
how many branches stripped
and nailed
to make each crucifix?

Goldwasser

The snowstorm
in this bottle
is purest gold,
as if the ceiling
of heaven
were flaking down,
as if a gold bird
trapped in the bottle
were beating its feathers
against the glass.
I tip
my head to drink,
and my throat
is flecked with gold,
my words
become valuable
they flash
like the gleam
of a gold-toothed
smile,
and I am changed,
a tiny sun explodes
behind each eye
its motes
come trembling
down,
I drink.
While somewhere
in Midas's kingdom
a peasant plowing
his necklace of earth
looks up to see
an ordinary day of snow—
the flakes
all newly minted
and clinking
as they fall.

Prosody 101

When they taught me that what mattered most
was not the strict iambic line goose-stepping
over the page but the variations
in that line and the tension produced
on the ear by the surprise of difference,
I understood yet didn't understand
exactly, until just now, years later
in spring, with the trees already lacy
and camellias blowsy with middle age
I looked out and saw what a cold front had done
to the garden, sweeping in like common language,
unexpected in the sensuous
extravagance of a Maryland spring.
There was a dark edge around each flower
as if it had been outlined in ink
instead of frost, and the tension I felt
between the expected and actual
was like that time I came to you, ready
to say goodbye for good, for you had been
a cold front yourself lately, and as I walked in
you laughed and lifted me up in your arms
as if I too were lacy with spring
instead of middle aged like the camellias,
and I thought: So this is Poetry.

In Early March

Those first Impressionists,
tracking light as if
it were an animal to catch
in nets of color,
or a tide that could be measured
on canvas instead of sand,
they knew what happens
in early March,
how the frozen page of earth
means nothing.
It is the light
that tells us
spring.

To the Field Goal Kicker in a Slump

It must be something
like writer's block,
when nothing will go
between the margins,
when language won't soar
high enough,
when you wake
in the morning and know
you've chosen
the wrong game.

The Writer at 16

He thinks of himself always
in the third person, an only
child of his own imagination,
gazing into his life
not with love or pity
but with a curiosity
in which he may almost
drown.

There is still
a mother there and a father,
the way the moon is there during
a partial eclipse of the sun,
but even the blue of the sky
can seem bruised
by his terrible
insights.

At night he looms
over the page, inventing
his muse, an older woman,
and in the explosive
silence of that house
he chews his pencils
as noisily as his watching sisters
chew their nails.

Orpheus

When Orpheus turned
and looked back and knew
that genius wasn't enough,
I wonder which he regretted most:
the failure of will,
Eurydice lost,
or what it must mean for her
to remain
a fraction of darkness?

Did he still tame animals
with his songs,
or would that seem a child's game now?
Did he tune his lyre
to a minor key,
the last notes falling
like darkened leaves
to drift towards Lesbos?

In Balanchine's ballet
the failure seems Eurydice's fault
who tempted his blindfold off,
as if the artist must be absolved,
as if what matters
is the body itself—
that instrument stringed
with tendon and bone
making its own music.

2. Dream Plants

Warm Front

The plum tree
in my garden
blooms today,
though it's December.
And the weathermen,
like defeated generals,
have folded their maps
and gone home.
There is no truth

a lawyer told me once,
just evidence.
What would he make
of this evidence
in my garden
of spring—
the only snow in sight
a handful of blossoms set loose
by the wind?

Green Thumb

No bigger than a thumb
and palest green,
a tree frog
has stowed away
on one of the plants
my husband brought inside
for winter,
and in the darkness
it fills the spaces
of this house
with disproportionate
song. The dogs bark,
fearing a creature
they cannot see,
and partly to quiet them
we search in vain
among the stems
and roots and leaves
for that balloon
of swollen sound—
either lovelorn,
or joyful, or hungry.
I'm never sure
I want the woods inside,
though circumscribed in pots
these plants seem safe enough—
contained explosions of green
at every frozen window.
Whatever my husband touches
grows. Tonight when he
touches me, black earth
still rings the moons
of all his nails.
I think it is a naked
infant's call
the tree frog's song
reminds me of.

Dream Plants

You give me fuchsias for my birthday,
their strange bell-like flowers
improbable shades of red,
the color of Buddhist temple bells.
These are dream plants—not quite nightmares
but those shadowy dreams left over from childhood
where terror and beauty mix
and the difference between plants and animals
is vaguer than we thought.

For your birthday I give books
I hope to read when you are finished,
though I know you'd rather be out
in the garden planting
than reading books.
I think gardens are for reading in,
a kind of background to please the eye
as the pages turn—a pause in mid-sentence
brief as a comma. So we try to give

our own lives to each other, to change
places a moment in the slow dance through time.
The plants you give me will make their way
to your desk; the books will be left
on my side of the bed. And we will look
at each other with an old promise
improbable as the reds of the fuchsias
or the intricate terror and beauty
I look for in books.

Lullabye for 17

You are so young
you heal as you weep,
and your tears
instead of scalding
your face like mine
absolve
simply as rain.

I tried to teach you
what I knew: how men
in their sudden beauty
are more dangerous,
how love refracting light
can burn the hand, how memory
is a scorpion

and stings with its tail.
You knew my catechism
but never believed. Now
you look upon pain
as a discovery all your own,
marveling at the way it invades
the bloodstream, ambushes sleep.

Still you forgive
so easily. I'd like
to take your young man
by his curls and tear
them out,
who like a dark planet circles
your bright universe

still furnished with curtains
you embroidered yourself,
an underbrush
of books and scarves,
a door at which
you'll soon be poised
to leave.

Last Will

Children,
when I am ash
read by the light of the fire
that consumes me
this document
whose subject is love.

I want to leave you everything: my life
divided into so many parts
there are enough to go around; the world
from this window: weather and a tree
which bequeaths
all of its leaves each year.

Today the lawyer plans
for your descendants,
telling a story
of generations
that seems to come true
even as he speaks.

My books will fill
your children's shelves,
my small enameled spoons
invade their drawers. It is
the only way I know, so far,
to haunt.

Let me be a guest at my own funeral
and at the reading of my will.
You I'll reward first
for the moments of your births,
those three brief instants
when I understood my life.

But wisdom bends as light does
around the objects it touches.
The only legacy you need was left
by accident long ago:
a secret in the genes.
The rest is small change.

Instructions for Decanting Wine

You must choose a bottle
that has been in repose
for a long time.
Then whisper this incantation:
Côte d'Or, Côte de Bordeaux,
Côte de Nuits. Now
carefully pour the wine
into a clear vessel.
The liquid should be
the color of sky
just before storm,
the color of your own mouth
bruised after love,
or after tasting the wild grapes
that grow in a tangle
by the locked door.
Beware of the fox.
Beware of the visions
wine may bring: a ridged shell
with Venus curled inside,
half sleeping.
As for the bottle itself,
never throw it away.
The sediment that clings
like barnacles
to its slippery sides
is the accretion of years
of fine detail . . . stitch,
syllable, hair . . .
it is what happens to memory
when the rememberer is gone.
But if you must,
throw the bottle far
into the sea,
which Homer called wine dark.
Years later, someone
you love will wait
for the message hidden inside
to wash up
in the intoxicated foam
at her once grape-stained
feet.

Prince Camille De Rohan
(hybrid perpetual, dark red shaded with maroon)

Sunned and pruned,
this Spanish
rose performs
its brilliant
death in the
arena
of high June,
its secret:
brevity
and a thorn—
red-caped and
dangerous
as any
matador's.

Coronary Bypass: for Rod

So now they've made a detour
to your heart, routed the blood
like traffic through a different place
past derelict scenery some call
inner landscape—those aging
monuments of bone and muscle.

Old friend, they've primed your pump
to beat its iambs out for years.
Next week you'll write
of tulips on the windowsill
heart-shaped and red
and drunk with oxygen.

root canal

under the anesthetic
tiny gondoliers
sing to me

pizzicato
and I am
borne away

helpless as
childhood
as they pole

through the shadowed
waters
of the mouth

Nostalgia

At the moment when memory dims
a whole octave, when the light
it throws backwards
becomes soft, a powdery light
blurring
the eye and dulling
the sharp blade of feeling—
at that moment we relinquish
our childhoods.

My dead father stands waving.
He has forgotten all my failures,
and under his black mustache surely he smiles.
My mother has left her mirror
and stands by the stove.
Around her cluster the sisters
and brothers I never had, though I leaned
out of an open window for years
calling their names.

Let the bare bones of fact
beat their terrible rhythms
elsewhere. On the Grand Concourse
the Bronx Bus stopped
and started all night,
but I only remember
a faithful beast
breathing
over my broken sleep.

Market Day

We have traveled all this way
to see the real France:
these trays of apricots and grapes spilled out
like semi-precious stones
for us to choose; a milky way
of cheeses whose names like planets
I forget; heraldic sole
displayed on ice, as if the fish
themselves had just escaped,
leaving their scaled armor behind.
There's nothing like this
anywhere, you say. And I see
Burnside Avenue in the Bronx, my mother

sending me for farmer cheese and lox:
the rounds of cheese grainy and white, pocked
like the surface of the moon;
the silken slices of smoked fish
lying in careful pleats; and always,
as here, sawdust under our feet
the color of sand brought in on pant cuffs
from Sunday at the beach.
Across the street on benches,
my grandparents lifted their faces
to the sun the way the blind turn
towards a familiar sound, speaking
another language I almost understand.

At the Train Museum

Topeka . . . Junction City . . .
Santa Fe. The places
the imagination takes us
are simply these.
All . . . Points . . . East
the conductor calls
in that old plainchant

and a girl with a suitcase
steals down the porch stairs.
Rivers . . . Bridges . . . Cornfields
with stalks as tasseled
as the plaited hair of children
all over Kansas, falling asleep
to the loon-like call

of trains. I board
one more time, sensing
the quicksilver tracks,
how they branch towards a future
where I've long since
been carried, swaying
and only half awake.

The Sonoran Desert, January

In this unfinished landscape
of space and sky
they tell me flowers will bloom later
and in strange colors, vivid
as fever dreams.

They tell me the saguaro cactus will seem
beautiful, that their creature shapes
are of this earth,
though they have the look
of another planet.

And the lizards, live outcroppings
of the rock,
the iguanas and horned toads
are also of this time,
this endless place.

Stay a while, they tell me.
The green hills back east
will seem as nothing
after these smoky hills.
The thirst you will learn here

is like no other thirst.
For the first time you will understand
what the sun—that burning thistle—asks
what water
so briefly answers.

Waiting for E. gularis

"An African heron was found on the northeast
 end of Nantucket Island . . ." news release

"The sighting of the century . . ." Roger Tory Peterson

Exile
by accident
he came

against
all instinct
to this watery place,

mistaking it
perhaps
as the explorers did

for some
new
Orient.

This morning,
dreaming
of the inexplicable

I rise from sleep, smoothing
the sheets behind me
to match

the water-smoothed sand
silk
under my bare feet.

I walk past morning joggers
who worship in pain
the crucible of breath,

past dune and marsh
stockaded with eel grass
to this pond,

just as a breeze comes up
like rumours
of his appearance.

Teenagers in bathing suits
lounge here, fans
waiting for their rock star

E. gularis—even his name
becomes
an incantation.

The pond
is all surface
this cloudy day,

the dark side of a mirror
where nothing shows
until you stare enough

as at those childhood puzzles—
how many faces can you find
concealed here?

And there moving towards us
is the turtle's miniature
face,

and there the mask
the wild duck wears, stitching
a ruffle

at the pond's far edge
where now
the Little Blue Herons

curve their necks
to question marks
(why not me?)

where in a semi-circle
ornithologists
wait

to add another notch
to their life
lists,

binoculars
raised
like pistols.

After Reading Peterson's Guide

I used to call them
Morning Doves, those birds
with breasts the rosy color
of dawn who coo us awake
as if to say love . . .
love . . . in the morning.

But when the book said
Mourning Doves instead,
I noticed their ash-gray feathers,
like shadows
on the underside
of love.

When the Dark Angel comes
let him fold us in wings
as soft as these birds',
though the speckled egg
hidden deep in his nest
is death.

Family Scene: Mid-Twentieth Century

In the photograph you and I sit together
with identical smiles,
each holding a dog by the collar;
the ocean is simply backdrop.
Marriage, could be the caption,
which frees and confines at the same time,
as those leashless dogs, now dead,
were checked by our hands on their collars.
It is probably just coincidence
that I found this photograph pressed
between pages of Tolstoy, though
I always said that you looked Russian—
Pierre, I suppose, not Vronsky, with your passion
for land and for growing.
Someone will find this picture
years from now and think:
mid-twentieth century, family scene,
people had pets instead of children.
Though of course we had children too
off somewhere, swimming perhaps
in that backdrop of water.
Who were we smiling for, ten years ago,
and what can we believe
if not our own faces in photos?
When you want to go faster, go slower!
a poet said, speaking of running marathons.
I want to go slower now, seeing only
darkness ahead, but you always hurry me on.
Didn't you rush us into this life together,
almost without thinking,
or at least holding our thoughts
the way we might hold our breath?
And didn't it all work out? you ask,
for there we are, twenty years into our marathon
caught in black and white and smiling,
and here we are now.
Dumb luck, my father would have said,
who never quite approved of you.
But who can ask for anything more of life
than those strategies of the genes
or the weather that we call luck?

September

it rained in my sleep
and in the morning the fields were wet

I dreamed of artillery
of the thunder of horses

in the morning the fields were strewn
with twigs and leaves

as if after a battle
or a sudden journey

I went to sleep in summer
I dreamed of rain

in the morning the fields were wet
and it was autumn

3. A Fraction of Darkness

Last Words

Let us consider
last words: Goethe's
"More Light," for instance,
or Gertrude Stein, sly
to the end, asking
"But what is the question?"

Consider the fisherman
caught on the hook
of his own death
who saves
his last words
for the sea.

Consider the miner,
the emblem of earth
on his face,
who curses the earth
as he enters it,
mineshaft or grave.

I have heard the dry sound
leaves make
on their way from the tree,
have felt the cold braille
of snow as it melts
in the hand.

It is almost time
to let the curtain
of darkness down
on the perfect exit,
to say one last time
a few loved names,

or else to go out
in silence
like an anonymous star
whose message,
if there is one,
is light years away.

Insomnia

At the rising of stars
the teeth of night
are set on edge,

at the rising of the moon
the earth changes from flesh
to bone.

We turn in bed
two dozen times
each hour,

the drowsing eyelid flickers
on and off
as if it had a loose connection.

This is the hour when doctors come
solemn as doormen
to usher a life in or out,

when even
the clock's face
is swept clean,

and lying here
I have lost
the passport to sleep.

Outside a season
is starting
or ending,

snow or rain
or leaves are waiting
to fall,

but the landscape
which I have always drawn up
under my chin

has been picked
bare
by years of weather.

It is not a failure
of love—you still
lie beside me,

but when I touch your wrist
I feel your pulse
unraveling.

How many paths I have followed
tracks and roadways leading to
this bed

where
if death
were the only sleep left

I would take his face
in my two hands
shyly

and drink with him
the steaming cup
of darkness.

Waiting Room

On line once, waiting
for a Greyhound bus
I stood behind a woman
with the same look
my father wore for weeks,
waiting to die.
And I thought
we practice
all our lives
waiting
on supermarket lines
burdened by produce,
by telephones
whose mute refusals
make silence
absolute;
we wait under clocks
with insect numbers
and arrows pointing
nowhere, in doctors' offices
thumbed over
like old magazines. Time is
the lover here, breathing
down your neck,
and when you need
him most, he'll disappear.
It was like this caught
in the shallows, waiting
to be born,
it is like this divided
among suitcases,
waiting to be left,
to leave. At home
waiting to grow up
I used to lean
against the sundial
my father built,
and the sun threw
its knife-edged
shadow down
cutting across
the knotted years.

Extremities

Yesterday I feared
the darkness
of the earth I must become,
the heaviness of earth
during that becoming.

Today I grieve
for the human curve
of hills
and the unlearned endings
of all the stories.

Which is worse, that fear
or this grieving?
I move between them
as I moved between
two hurts

when as a child
I dug my nails into the palm
of my right hand,
drawing blood, to fool
the broken bone in the left.

Routine Mammogram

We are looking for a worm
in the apple—
that fruit which ever since Eden

has been susceptible
to frost
or appetite.

The doctor shows me
aerial photographs,
moonscapes

of craters and lakes,
faults in the surface
I might fall through one day

valleys where every shadow
could mean total
eclipse.

This is just a base line, he says
as if my body were a camp
you could start climbing from.

In the mountains
they dream of snow and listen
for avalanche.

I think of Amazon women
with just one
breast,

their bowstrings
tightening
for war.

(How will we
ever
touch again?)

46

You're fine, the doctor
tells me now and smiles,
as if he could give innocence back,

as if he could give back
to the apple
its spiraled skin.

At My Desk: to Bill Stafford

How many times
I have sat this way
with the poem's intractable silence
between me and the world,
with the tree outside the window
refusing translation:
my leaves are more than syllables
it seems to say.

I think of you
miles west
floating on the tide of language
so easily, giving only
a scissors kick now and then,
coming to shore
some unexpected
but hospitable place.

Still we share between us
a certain stubbornness,
rising each morning
to the blank page,
climbing the ladder of light
at the window all day,
listening, both of us,
as hard as we can.

Departures

They seemed to all take off
at once: Aunt Grace
whose kidneys closed shop;
Cousin Rose who fed sugar
to diabetes;
my grandmother's friend
who postponed going so long
we thought she'd stay.

It was like the summer years ago
when they all set out on trains
and ships, wearing hats with veils
and the proper gloves,
because everybody was going
someplace that year,
and they didn't want
to be left behind.

In the Absence of Wings

"And look, Daedalus still
 hasn't invented
 the wings."
                    Miroslav Holub

Somewhere, a gardener
translates the labyrinth
into a maze of hawthorn and yew,

and though the minotaur sleeps,
the hawthorn is sharp
as a rosebush,

the yewberries
are bright
with poison.

It is evening.
I have watched the children wander off
into their lives,

I have locked the door
of my father's grave
behind me.

Soon I will finish with books,
their chaste
and voluptuous music.

Snow
and flowers alternate,
flowers and snow.

What I was given
has been taken
back,

what was withheld
I still
long for.

The horizon is the thread
I must tie to my wrist
in the absence

of wings, as I come
to the vine-scrolled gatepost
of the labyrinth.

Low Tide

At low tide
when the waves are spent,
I gather the intricate shells
my life has left
behind—all whorls
and darkened crevices.
I string them into a necklace
to wear for famished
memory's sake.

It is too late now
for the passionate guest
who would inhabit this flesh,
room by half-lit room;
too late
for a child
to hoist itself
up the slippery umbilical
towards the light.

Low tide; the moon is anchored
far to the west. At all
the outposts of my body
the driftwood fires
burn down,
and a stranger stands
shooting a perfect
arc of urine
into the ashes.

The Seven Deadly Sins

Avarice

They say that Midas
died a ruined man—
you can't eat gold,
gold can't keep you warm.
But that's just
allegory, and anyway
times have
changed. Give me
that touch.
I'll take my chances.

Pride

I have swallowed it
and swallowed it,
but I am like the Whale,
I can feel my Jonah
down there, waiting.
When I spit him out
everyone
will take notice.

Gluttony

As I finish lunch
I am thinking about
what I will eat
for dinner, so
if I give you
the smaller portion
of dessert, it is only
because I am
preoccupied. Here,
let's cover it
with cream.

Lust

There is a candle lit
between my thighs.
Come, blow it out,
you with the down
so new on your face
it could be a girl's,
though I saw the muscles quicken
under your shirt,
as my pulse
quickened when
you lifted the groceries
into my car.

Sloth

The indolent sloth
has three toes
on each front foot,
a small mammal, slow moving
and from . . .
South America.
Since you ask,
I would tell you which country,
but I am too tired
to look it up.

Envy

There was a green
silk scarf with gold
around the edges
that matched
my cousin's green eyes
flecked with gold.
Mother said mine
was pure merino wool.
Mother said never mind,
boys would want to marry
girls like me.

Anger

You tell me
that it's all right
to let it out of its cage,
though it may claw someone,
even bite.
You say that letting it out
may tame it somehow.
But loose it may
turn on me, maul
my face, draw blood.
Ah, you think you know so much,
you whose anger is a pet dog,
its canines dull with disuse.
But mine is a rabid thing,
sharpening its teeth
on my very bones,
and I will never let it go.

The Survivors

All savor gone,
the waves break saltless
on a bland shore.
Tears taste of chalk.
There is no prick of grass or weed
to make the numbed eye blink.
Not even the color of fire
remains. Here where sin
has hardly left a dust
the few survivors sit.
They see the clouds
barely move. They see
an animal so starved for salt
it licks the twisted body
of Lot's wife—
their only standing monument.

Remission

It seems you must grow
into your death slowly,
as if it were a pair of new shoes
waiting on the closet floor,
smelling of the animal
it came from, but still too big
too stiff for you to wear.
Meanwhile you dance barefoot
your shaky dance of pretence,
and we dance with you,
the pulses in our own wrists
ticking away.
In this small truce
the body waits,
having waged war on itself
for years. You say
the water tastes of flowers.
You steal on tiptoe
past the closet door.

Duet for One Voice

1.

I sit at your side
watching the tides of consciousness
move in and out, watching
the nurses, their caps
like so many white gulls circling
the bed. The window
grows slowly dark,
and light again,
and dark. The clock
tells the same old stories.
Last week you said, now
you'll have to learn
to sew for yourself.
If the thread is boredom,
the needle is grief.
I sit here learning.

2.

In place of spring
I offer this branch
of forsythia
whose yellow blossoms
I have forced.
Your tired mouth
forces a smile
in thanks. Outside
it is still cold;
who knows how long
the cold will last?
But underground,
their banners still furled,
whole armies of flowers wait.

3.

I am waiting for you to die,
even as I try to coax you
back to life
with custards and soup
and colored pills I shake
from the bottle like dice,
though their magic
went out of the world
with my surgeon father,
the last magician.
I am waiting

for you to be again
what you always were,
for you to be there whole
for me to run to with this new grief—
your death—the hair grown back
on your skull the way it used to be,
your widow's peak the one sure landmark
on the map of my childhood,
those years when I believed
that medicine and love and being good
could save us all.

4.

We escape from our mothers
again and again, young
Houdinis, playing the usual matinées.
First comes escape down
the birth canal, our newly carved faces
leading the way like figureheads
on ancient slaveships,
our small hands rowing for life.
Later escape into silence, escape
behind slammed doors,
the flight into marriage.
I thought I was finally old enough
to sit with you, sharing a book.
But when I look up
from the page, you
have escaped from me.

Clinic

In the perfect Democracy
of illness, we stand on line
for X-ray and EKG,
dressing and undressing,
clutching the charts
which slowly accumulate—
the only autobiography
we have left.

When did we stop
being part of our bodies
and start simply
to inhabit them,
the way we'd inhabit a house
that is not of our choosing,
and where, anyway, the rent
is due?

So who can blame the man
who threw his sonogram into the air
like so much ticker tape at a parade,
saying to Hell with it,
telling God just to take him,
and out of doors please, the way lightning
may take what is left of a tree
and make a skeleton out of it?

What We Look at Last

What if it's true
that what we look at last
in life
remains engraved forever
on our closed lids,
a miniature oval to fit the eye
like one of those tiny portraits
framed in gold leaf
my grandmother kept
on her mantel?

Did my father staring
at the hospital ceiling
as he died
have only that map
of cracked plaster
to follow
forever,
and where
can such accidental
signposts lead?

When I travel by air
I refuse all trays and magazines.
I gaze at acres
of furrowed cloud—
our guess of heaven.
Or far below I see
a speck of lighted window,
someone hidden behind it
with flowers perhaps, and bread
and candles for my unshriven feet.

Notes for an Elegy: for John Gardner

Because you died in autumn
I write
as though the leaves
had turned for you,

as though the sun's defection
on this chilly day
were somehow
particular.

I want to write condolence notes
not to your friends
but to the ones
who didn't know you yet.

I'd tell them how you'd give
a rough pat to the dog,
the backhand of attention to a thousand things,
how that sufficed.

Because your vivid life
was the continuous dream
of fiction, is death
a kind of waking up?

Did recklessness get you after all?
I used to picture you years from now
typing your way to old age
through the restless nights

the way you typed
that summer
in the room under mine
when I followed

the clattering footsteps
of your old machine
all the way
to sleep.

The Death of a Parent

Move to the front
of the line
a voice says, and suddenly
there is nobody
left standing between you
and the world, to take
the first blows
on their shoulders.
This is the place in books
where part one ends, and
part two begins,
and there is no part three.
The slate is wiped
not clean but like a canvas
painted over in white
so that a whole new landscape
must be started,
bits of the old
still showing underneath—
those colors sadness lends
to a certain hour of evening.
Now the line of light
at the horizon
is the hinge between earth
and heaven, only visible
a few moments
as the sun drops
its rusted padlock
into place.

Shadows

Each night this house sinks into the shadows
under its weight of love and fear and pity.
Each morning it floats up again so lightly
it seems attached to sky instead of earth,
a place where we will always go on living
and there will be no dead to leave behind.

But when we think of whom we've left behind
already in the ever-hungry shadows,
even in the morning hum of living
we pause a minute and are filled with pity
for the lovely children of the earth
who run up and down the stairs so lightly

and who weave their careless songs so lightly
through the hedges which they play behind
that the fruits and flowers of the earth
rise up on their stems above the shadows.
Perhaps even an apple can feel pity;
perhaps the lilac wants to go on living.

In this house where we have all been living
we bind the family together lightly
with knots made equally of love and pity
and the knowledge that we'll leave behind
only partial memories, scraps of shadows,
trinkets of our years upon the earth.

I think about my father in the earth
as if it were a room in which he's living,
as if it were a house composed of shadows
where he remembers those he loved not lightly,
where he remembers what he left behind.
He had a great capacity for pity

but told me that I mustn't waste my pity
on him—he'd had his share of life on earth,
and he was happy just to leave behind
daughters of daughters who would go on living.
So he seemed to leave us almost lightly,
closing the curtains which were stitched with shadows.

Always save your pity for the living
who walk the eggshell crust of earth so lightly,
in front of them, behind them, only shadows.